THE SCIENCE OF
FOOTBALL

THE TOP 10 WAYS SCIENCE AFFECTS THE GAME

by Greg Nicolai

Consultant:
Harold Pratt
President of Educational Consultants
Littleton, Colorado

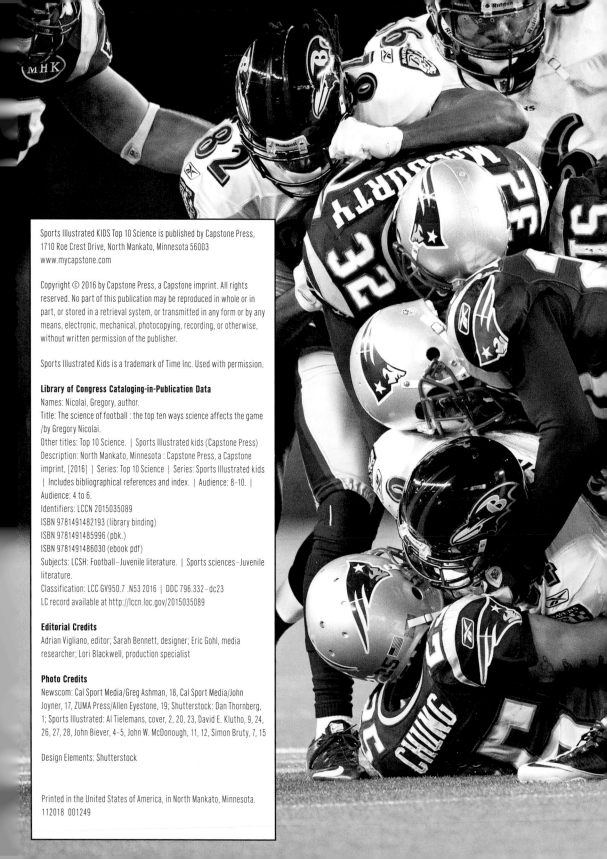

Sports Illustrated KIDS Top 10 Science is published by Capstone Press,
1710 Roe Crest Drive, North Mankato, Minnesota 56003
www.mycapstone.com

Library of Congress Cataloging-in-Publication Data
Names: Nicolai, Gregory, author.
Title: The science of football : the top ten ways science affects the game
/by Gregory Nicolai.
Other titles: Top 10 Science. | Sports Illustrated kids (Capstone Press)
Description: North Mankato, Minnesota : Capstone Press, a Capstone
imprint, [2016] | Series: Top 10 Science | Series: Sports Illustrated kids
| Includes bibliographical references and index. | Audience: 8-10. |
Audience: 4 to 6.
Identifiers: LCCN 2015035089
ISBN 9781491482193 (library binding)
ISBN 9781491485996 (pbk.)
ISBN 9781491486030 (ebook pdf)
Subjects: LCSH: Football—Juvenile literature. | Sports sciences—Juvenile
literature.
Classification: LCC GV950.7 .N53 2016 | DDC 796.332—dc23
LC record available at http://lccn.loc.gov/2015035089

Editorial Credits
Adrian Vigliano, editor; Sarah Bennett, designer; Eric Gohl, media
researcher; Lori Blackwell, production specialist

Photo Credits
Newscom: Cal Sport Media/Greg Ashman, 18, Cal Sport Media/John
Joyner, 17, ZUMA Press/Allen Eyestone, 19; Shutterstock: Dan Thornberg,
1; Sports Illustrated: Al Tielemans, cover, 2, 20, 23, David E. Klutho, 9, 24,
26, 27, 28, John Biever, 4-5, John W. McDonough, 11, 12, Simon Bruty, 7, 15

Design Elements: Shutterstock

Printed in the United States of America, in North Mankato, Minnesota.
112018   001249

Table of Contents

The fans have passed through the gates of the stadium and found their seats in the autumn sunshine. Despite the chill in the air, some fans have painted their chests with team colors. As the players take their positions for the opening kickoff, the roar of the crowd surges toward the field. The players have to shout to hear one another. After a toot of the ref's whistle, the kicker launches the ball from the tee and into the sky. The receiving team waits as the ball falls end over end and lands in the sure hands of the returner while the kicking team charges forward, hoping for a quick tackle.

The game has begun. Behind all of the excitement and emotion, the principles of science determine everything that happens on the field. From the tight spiral of a pinpoint pass to the collision of running back and linebacker, football is a game of physics.

Shooting Spirals

The tight spiral of a perfect pass is one of football's most beautiful sights. The ball seems to shoot through the air as if nothing were affecting its movement. But air pressure does push on the ball, just as gravity constantly pulls on it. It is the way the quarterback throws the ball, spinning it quickly along its width, which allows the ball to move through the air so smoothly.

During the game Atlanta Falcons quarterback Matt Ryan probably isn't thinking about physics concepts, but he has learned how to use these principles. When releasing the ball, Ryan rotates it from the outside down toward the ground while projecting the ball forward. This force creates a rotating movement.

Whenever an object moves through the air, air pushes back on the object and creates **friction**. Friction can make the object wobble. A spiraling football does not wobble because the tight rotation of the ball reduces friction. Instead of the air pressing on the football and pushing it this way and that, the air is swept evenly around the ball's length, allowing the ball to fly with ease.

friction ⟼ a force produced when two objects rub against each other

A tight spiral helps Matt Ryan keep each pass as accurate as possible.

7

Running the Routes

During a game, receivers bolt from the line of scrimmage and take complex paths in their search for open space and the possibility of a catch. This requires skill and the ability to follow passing routes. Passing routes are planned ahead of time to give a receiver the best chance to avoid defenders and open up a passing lane for the quarterback.

A stop-and-go route is meant to trick the defender by placing him in an awkward position in which he is unable to catch up with the receiver. Green Bay Packers wide receiver Jordy Nelson sprints about 10 yards down the field and then abruptly stops and turns toward the quarterback. This is meant to get the defender to also stop in order to break up the pass. Nelson then resumes his sprint up the field leaving the defender behind him. What makes this route successful is that Nelson knows the actual route while the defender doesn't know when the pass might come. This gives Nelson a slight advantage in timing.

▸ A well-run passing route gives Jordy Nelson the best chance to haul in a big catch.

It takes a runner time to move from a dead stop to full speed. This is the principle of **acceleration**. If a stop-and-go route fools a defender as planned, the receiver will have a few moments to accelerate while the defender is at a dead stop. By the time the defender begins to accelerate again the receiver will have reached his top speed, giving the defender less of a chance of catching up.

acceleration ⟹ the change in the velocity of a body

Changing Direction

One of the attractions of football is its combination of hard-hitting action and fast-moving players. But the use of speed in the game is a bit more complicated than a player simply running as fast as he can. If Seattle Seahawks running back Marshawn Lynch finds an open field in front of him, he can race at top speed to get to the goal line. During most running plays, however, Lynch must adjust his speed to avoid tackles and find open running lanes.

As a player's speed increases, it is more difficult for him to change his direction. English physicist Sir Isaac Newton's first law of motion says that objects at rest stay at rest and objects in motion stay in motion in a straight line, unless an outside force acts on them. The faster an object moves, the greater the force required to change its direction. During a running play, Lynch plans to change direction quickly to gain the most yards possible. Instead of sprinting, Lynch anticipates changing directions and will usually vary his speed to make himself more nimble.

▼ Marshawn Lynch combines speed, power, and agility to gain as many yards as possible with every run.

Rising Above the Competition

For a receiver to make a catch, he must have precise control of his body. When a high pass flies in near the sideline, Dallas Cowboys wide receiver Dez Bryant leaps up above nearby defenders to catch the ball while staying in the same space on the field.

To get the most out of his vertical leap, Bryant must use his leg muscles to create enough force to push away from the ground. First, Bryant must create a firm grip on the turf. His cleats allow him to dig into the turf, creating greater surface area and friction. This lets him use the force of his leg muscles against the ground. He first bends his knees then forcefully straightens his legs, producing **kinetic energy** in the motion of his body.

This series of movements is similar to compressing a spring then suddenly converting the energy stored in the compressed spring to kinetic energy by letting the spring loose. Bryant uses this energy to push against the constant force of gravity and leap into the air. With the right amount of force applied to a jump, Bryant can bring his hands up to meet the ball for a perfect catch beyond the defender's grasp.

kinetic energy ➡ the energy in a moving object due to its mass and velocity

The Art of the Tackle

Collision Force

As the center snaps the ball to the quarterback, both teams explode into action. The quarterback drops back and looks for an open receiver as the offensive line struggles to hold off the defenders. Suddenly, Houston Texans defensive end J. J. Watt crashes through the line and slams into the quarterback, bringing him down for a sack. Tackling happens so quickly that it can be easy to miss the details, which make powerful use of the principles of physics.

One of the main concepts involved with tackling is **momentum**, which is the **mass** of an object multiplied by its **velocity**. Basically, the bigger something is and the faster it moves, the greater an impact it can make when it hits something. That's why a player's speed and size are so important in football. Defensive ends like Watt increase their velocity before a tackle, using any available time and space to create as much momentum as possible. If Watt creates greater momentum than that of the player he's trying to tackle, he has a better chance of bringing down his opponent. If Watt's momentum is less than his opponent's, he is less likely to succeed.

momentum ➡ a property of a moving object determined by multiplying its mass and velocity

mass ➡ the amount of material in an object

velocity ➡ a measurement of both the speed and direction an object is moving

▲ The sight of J. J. Watt breaking through the offensive line is bad news for any quarterback.

Liftoff

In addition to creating huge momentum, tacklers must use good technique to control their tackles. When Carolina Panthers linebacker Luke Kuechly goes for a tackle, he hits the ball carrier low and tries to drive up and through the tackle. Kuechly tries to keep his **center of gravity** lower than that of the ball carrier while using the momentum of his body to spring up into the ball carrier. By doing this, Kuechly generates force by pushing against the ground and up through the ball carrier, lifting the opponent off his feet.

Powerful tackles are exciting to watch, but they can also be dangerous for the players involved. Players' pads and helmets are designed to work together to make tackles safer. When Kuechly collides with an opponent, force is applied to the parts of both players' bodies that come into contact. Without pads, that force would be absorbed only by the players' muscles, bones, and ligaments. Instead, the pads and helmets help to absorb and redistribute the force of the tackle over a large area. By the time the force reaches a player's body, it isn't concentrated in one spot, reducing the chance of injury.

center of gravity ➟ the point on an object at which it can balance

Luke Kuechly stays low to give himself the best chance of making a successful tackle. ▼

momentum

TACKLING TECHNIQUE

Even with protective gear, players risk harm on every play. While the technology behind the equipment continues to improve, good tackling technique can also help to reduce the chance of injury. By staying low and leading with the shoulders rather than the head, the chance of head injuries can be reduced.

Holding the Line

Football players must be both strong and quick. This applies not only to running backs and linebackers, but to linemen as well. When the center snaps the ball, Cleveland Browns offensive tackle Joe Thomas collides with the defense. Thomas uses his strength and size to stop defensive linemen and blitzing linebackers from reaching the backfield. But Thomas also has quick feet that allow him to change his position in an instant in order to block off any surprise moves meant to get past him.

SWIM MOVE

When a defensive player meets an offensive lineman he may attempt a swim move. The defender starts by jabbing the lineman's shoulders to push him off-balance. Then the defender fakes to one side before moving quickly to the other. At the same time, he uses one arm to pull the lineman forward while "swimming" his other arm over the lineman's head. This allows the defender an open path to the quarterback or running back. But if the offensive lineman has quick feet and a low center of mass, he has a better chance of staying in front of the defender and blocking the swim move.

Thomas starts each play by lowering his **center of mass**. The rest of the offensive and defensive linemen do the same, crouching low so they can stay stable when crashing into one another. The higher a player's center of mass is, the easier it will be for another player to move or even to topple him over.

◄ Joe Thomas must position his center of mass to keep himself stable so he can provide solid protection on every play.

center of mass ⇒ the point in a body at which most of the mass appears to be concentrated

Protect Your Head

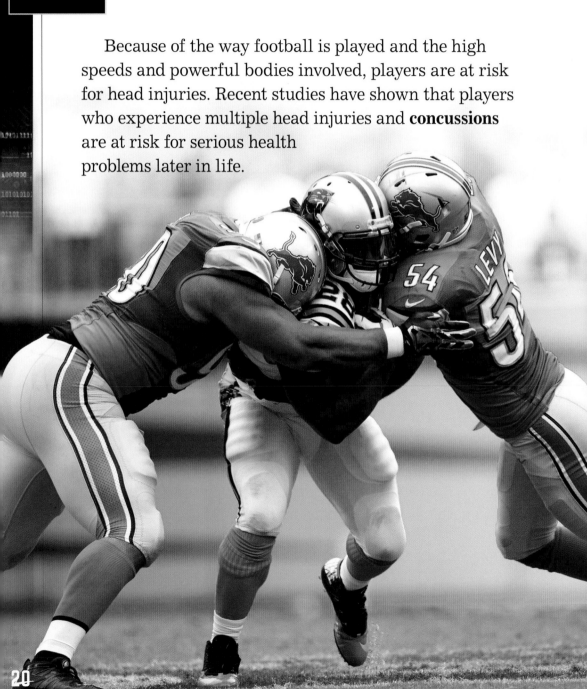

Because of the way football is played and the high speeds and powerful bodies involved, players are at risk for head injuries. Recent studies have shown that players who experience multiple head injuries and **concussions** are at risk for serious health problems later in life.

A concussion occurs when a hard blow to the head causes the brain to slam against the skull. In football this can happen in a tackle or any time when two players, both moving at high speeds, collide. According to Newton's first law of motion, an object in motion will stay in motion in a straight line until acted upon by an outside force. When the impact of a tackle causes a player's body to stop moving forward, the player's internal organs are still in motion. If enough force is involved, this can cause the brain to hit the inside of the skull.

Seattle Seahawks coach Pete Carroll has turned to rugby, a relative of football, for help in developing safer tackling. Because rugby players don't wear helmets, they have learned safer tackling techniques than those traditionally used in football. Carroll trains his players to tackle like rugby players by leading with a shoulder. When a defender keeps his head to the side and uses his shoulders, arms, and legs to create the force of the tackle, concussions are less likely to occur.

HELMET-TO-HELMET

In the NFL, it is illegal for a player to tackle while leading with his head. Penalties are often given if a defender leads with his head and creates helmet-to-helmet contact while tackling. Helmet-to-helmet tackling is very dangerous because it can cause especially violent blows to a player's head and may result in injury.

concussion ⇒ an injury to the brain caused by a hard blow to the head

Through the Uprights

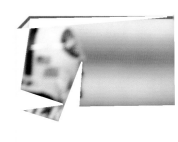

When Indianapolis Colts placekicker Adam Vinatieri prepares for a field goal attempt, he follows an exact routine. Vinatieri starts at the ball and paces backward to the starting point in order to ensure a precise kick. Few things in football require such careful preparation as the long-distance field goal.

As Vinatieri runs toward the ball, he increases his momentum. This helps him transfer more energy to the ball, allowing it to move faster and farther. At the right moment, Vinatieri plants his non-kicking foot into the ground as his kicking leg begins swinging toward the ball. He keeps a slight bend in the knee of his kicking leg until the last moment.

As Vinatieri's foot connects with the ball, his kicking leg snaps straight. This snapping motion allows him to transfer extra energy into the ball, creating a more powerful kick. To finish the kick, Vinatieri lets his leg continue its swing as the ball sails toward the goalposts.

▲ The precision of their job requires placekickers to stay calm and focused under pressure.

WEATHER CONDITIONS

Air pressure and temperature affect how a ball must be kicked. The warmer or higher above sea level air is, the less dense it becomes. Because air creates friction on a football, a ball kicked through less dense air faces less resistance and can travel farther.

Wind also makes demands on a kicker's ability. Kicking with the wind will allow the ball to travel farther, while kicking into the wind requires a more forceful kick. If the wind is blowing across the field, a kicker must not kick directly at his target, but rather into the wind so that the ball will be pushed to where he wants it to land.

Precision Punts

With three yards to go on fourth down, the San Diego Chargers bring punter Mike Scifres onto the field. Scifres' task is more challenging than a placekick in some ways. He must catch the snap and kick the ball away quickly, all while the defense charges at him. He must precisely drop the ball into a kick that produces the best punt for the situation.

Once Scifres receives the long snap, he has time to take two quick steps before punting. These few steps must generate velocity to transfer momentum to the punt and increase its speed and distance. After two steps, Scifres gently releases the ball. His leg is already swinging forward to make contact. Seconds before the sprinting defenders reach him, Scifres kicks the ball with the top of his foot.

As the ball sails through the air, it rotates along its axis backward toward Scifres. This rotational motion makes it more difficult for the punt returner to catch the ball. Because the punt is well placed, the returner decides not to attempt a catch. The ball lands on the ground, bouncing up and away from the end zone due to its rotational motion. Scifres' teammates arrive seconds later, downing the ball to pin their opponents back in their own zone.

◀ A punter does not kick from a stationary tee or have a holder to position the ball for him.

The 12th Man

Crowd Noise

As the Kansas City Chiefs defense takes the field, the home fans shake Arrowhead Stadium with a huge roar. A Chiefs defender raises his arms, encouraging home fans to cheer even louder to make things as difficult as possible for the visiting offense. Later, when the Chiefs are on offense, the crowd quiets down so that the quarterback can communicate. Fans make as much noise as possible, hoping to encourage the home team and intimidate the visiting team. This is fun for the fans, but it also serves a practical purpose.

Football is a sport of strategy with complex plays. Offenses often need to change plays at the last second as the quarterback reads the defensive formation. These quick play changes, called audibles, require communication. Crowd noise can interfere with that communication.

◀ A loud home crowd can help their team by disrupting the visiting team's offensive communication.

Stadium Design

A stadium's design has an effect on the way the sound of the crowd behaves. In a "bowl" style stadium, the cheering crowd's sound waves reflect off of the opposite stands and create added noise. In a stadium with open ends, more of those sound waves escape into the outside world. However, in a closed stadium such as the Detroit Lions' Ford Field, there is nowhere for the sound to go. The crowd's cheers bounce off of the walls and ceiling creating an echo effect that can raise the sound to ear-splitting levels. In addition, hard surfaces in a stadium such as concrete and metal reflect more sound than softer material would, adding to the effect.

▲ An enclosed stadium can amplify the effects of crowd noise.

Whether it's a running back darting through oncoming defenders or a linebacker delivering a crushing sack, football superstars all rely on science as part of their on-field success. Each pass, kick, and tackle is both a skill and a science. So the next time you're watching your favorite team take the field, consider the science behind their success!

WORLD-RECORD RACKET

Dome stadiums have the potential to be loudest, but crowd noise also depends on how loud the fans themselves can get. Two open-air stadiums are currently the loudest in the NFL. Fans of the Kansas City Chiefs at Arrowhead Stadium set the world record for crowd roar on September 29, 2014. The noise was recorded at 142.2 **decibels** (dB). This beat the previous record of 137.6 dB set by fans of the Seattle Seahawks at CenturyLink Field on December 2, 2013.

decibel ⇒ a unit for measuring how loud a sound is

GLOSSARY

acceleration (ak-sel-uh-RAY-shuhn) ➡ the change in the velocity of a body

center of gravity (SEN-tur UHV GRAV-uh-tee) ➡ the point on an object at which it can balance

center of mass (SEN-tur UHV MASS) ➡ the point in a body at which most of the mass appears to be concentrated

concussion (kuhn-KUH-shuhn) ➡ an injury to the brain caused by a hard blow to the head

decibel (DE-suh-buhl) ➡ a unit for measuring how loud a sound is

friction (FRIK-shuhn) ➡ a force produced when two objects rub against each other; friction slows down objects.

kinetic energy (ki-NET-ik EN-ur-jee) ➡ the energy in a moving object due to its mass and velocity

mass (MASS) ➡ the amount of material in an object

momentum (moh-MEN-tuhm) ➡ a property of a moving object determined by multiplying its mass and velocity

velocity (vuh-LOSS-uh-tee) ➡ a measurement of both the speed and direction an object is moving

READ MORE

Bethea, Nikole Brooks. *The Science of Football with Max Axiom, Super Scientist*. North Mankato, Minn.: Capstone Press, 2016.

Frederick, Shane. *Football: The Math of the Game*. Mankato, Minn.: Capstone Press, 2012.

Nagelhout, Ryan. *The Science of Football*. New York: PowerKids Press, 2016.

INTERNET SITES

FactHound offers a safe, fun way to find Internet sites related to this book. All of the sites on FactHound have been researched by our staff.

Here's all you do:

Visit *www.facthound.com*

Type in this code: 9781491482193

Check out projects, games and lots more at
www.capstonekids.com

INDEX